Let's Get

TAPAS

Over **100** Spanish dishes

*igloo*books

Published in 2017
by Igloo Books Ltd
Cottage Farm
Sywell
NN6 0BJ
www.igloobooks.com

Designed by Nicholas Gage
Edited by Jasmin Peppiatt

All imagery © iStock / Getty Images

LEO002 0717
2 4 6 8 10 9 7 5 3 1
ISBN 978-1-78557-500-6

Printed and manufactured in China

Contents

Cosas de Picar

(Finger Food)

Smoked Salmon and Caper Montaditos

8 slices granary baguette
150 g / 5 ½ oz / ⅔ cup cream cheese
50 g / 1 ¾ oz / ¼ cup baby
  capers, drained
4 slices smoked salmon, halved
1 lemon, zest finely pared
a few sprigs of dill

1. Arrange the baguette slices on a serving plate.
2. Mix the cream cheese with the capers and spread it on the baguette slices.
3. Top each one with half a slice of smoked salmon, a sprinkle of lemon zest and a frond of dill.

MAKES: 8 | PREP TIME: 10 MINS

Goat's Cheese and Walnut Montaditos

8 slices crusty baguette
4 batavia lettuce leaves, halved
8 slices soft goat's cheese log
8 slices roasted red pepper in oil, drained
50 g / 1 ¾ oz / ½ cup walnuts, chopped
1 tbsp runny honey
a pinch of cayenne pepper
8 sprigs parsley

1. Arrange the baguette slices on a serving plate and top each one with half a lettuce leaf.
2. Lay the goat's cheese on top, followed by the peppers.
3. Mix the walnuts with the honey and cayenne and spoon a little onto each montadito. Garnish each one with a small sprig of parsley.

Galician Octopus

3 bay leaves
1 garlic bulb, halved horizontally
1 tbsp sea salt
1 octopus, frozen for at least 2 weeks
    and defrosted
4 medium waxy potatoes
3 tbsp olive oil
1 tsp smoked paprika

1. Bring a large saucepan of water to the boil and add the bay leaf, garlic and salt.
2. Submerge the octopus and simmer for 30 minutes.
3. Add the potatoes to the pan and simmer for a further 20 minutes or until the potatoes and octopus are tender to the point of a knife.
4. Drain well, then peel and slice the potatoes and arrange on a large serving platter.
5. Slice the octopus (discarding the eyes and beak) and arrange on top, then drizzle with oil and sprinkle with paprika.
6. Serve warm for the best texture.

Pumpkin and Goat's Cheese Montaditos

175 g / 6 oz / 1 ½ cups pumpkin or
    butternut squash, diced
8 slices granary baguette
150 g / 5 ½ oz / ⅔ cup soft goat's cheese
1 tsp sesame seeds
1 tsp golden linseeds
1 tsp hemp seeds
1 tbsp fresh oregano leaves

1. Steam the pumpkin for 15 minutes or until tender. Leave to cool.
2. Arrange the baguette slices on a serving plate and spread with goat's cheese.
3. Top with the diced pumpkin and sprinkle with seeds and oregano.

Carne Fresca Montaditos

350 g / 12 oz / 2 ⅓ cups fillet steak
½ red onion, finely chopped
2 tsp sherry vinegar
100 g / 3 ½ oz / ⅔ cup green olives, pitted
3 tbsp capers
1 clove of garlic, crushed
2 tbsp basil leaves, finely chopped
2 tbsp olive oil
12 slices baguette

1. Cut the beef into very thin slices with a sharp knife, then cut each slice into a fine julienne. Cut across the julienne strips into tiny squares then mix with the onion and sherry vinegar. Season to taste with salt and white pepper.
2. Put the olives, capers, garlic, basil and oil in a mini food processor and pulse until finely chopped and evenly mixed.
3. Arrange the baguette slices on a serving platter and divide the steak mixture between them.
4. Top each montadito with a spoonful of tapenade and serve immediately.

Crispy Butterflied Prawns

18 raw king prawns, peeled with tails
   left intact
4 tbsp plain (all purpose) flour
1 egg, beaten
75 g / 2 ½ oz / ¾ cup panko breadcrumbs
sunflower oil, for deep-frying
lemon wedges and chilli (chili) sauce,
   to serve

1. Carefully slice down the back of the prawns, without cutting all the way through, and remove the black intestinal track. Open them up and pat down gently with your hand to butterfly them.
2. Dip the prawns alternately in the flour, egg and breadcrumbs. Shake off any excess.
3. Heat the oil in a deep fat fryer, according to the manufacturer's instructions, to a temperature of 180°C (350F).
4. Lower the prawns in the fryer basket and cook for 3 minutes or until crisp and golden brown.
5. Tip the prawns into a kitchen paper lined bowl to remove any excess oil. Serve immediately, with lemon wedges and chilli sauce on the side.

SERVES: **4** | PREP TIME: **25 MINS** | COOKING TIME: **3 MINS**

Salmon and Spinach Bites

1 tbsp olive oil
4 spring onions (scallions), chopped
1 clove of garlic, crushed
100 g / 3 ½ oz / 3 cups baby
  spinach, washed
400 g / 14 oz / 2 ⅔ cups skinless, boneless
  salmon, cut into chunks
sunflower oil, for deep frying
aioli, to serve

1. Heat the olive oil in a sauté pan and fry the spring onions and garlic for 3 minutes. Pack the spinach into the pan and put on the lid. Steam for 3 minutes, then remove the lid and stir-fry until well wilted. Leave to cool.
2. Put the salmon and spinach in a food processor with a big pinch of salt and pulse until finely chopped and sticky.
3. Heat the oil in a deep fat fryer, according to the manufacturer's instructions, to a temperature of 180°C (350F).
4. Use a small ice cream scoop to portion the mixture into balls and drop them straight into the hot oil. Fry the fish balls in batches for 3 minutes or until they are golden brown, turning over halfway through.
5. Line a large bowl with a few layers of kitchen paper and when they are ready, tip them into the bowl to remove any excess oil.
6. Serve immediately with aioli for dipping.

MAKES: **6** | PREP TIME: **10 MINS** | COOKING TIME: **25 MINS**

Stuffed Mushrooms

6 portabella mushrooms, stalks removed
1 tomato, diced
½ onion, diced
100 g / 3 ½ oz / 1 cup cheese, grated
2 tbsp flat leaf parsley, chopped
50 ml / 1 ¾ fl. oz / ¼ cup olive oil

1. Preheat the oven to 200°C (180°C fan) / 400F / gas 6.
2. Arrange the mushrooms, open side up, in a roasting tin.
3. Mix the tomato with the onion, cheese and parsley and stuff the mushrooms with the mixture. Drizzle the mushrooms with oil and season with salt and pepper.
4. Bake the mushrooms for 25 minutes or until tender to the point of a knife. Serve immediately.

Sundried Tomato and Ham Montaditos

8 slices cheese baguette

100 g / 3 ½ oz / ½ cup soft goat's cheese

150 g / 5 ½ oz / 1 cup sundried tomatoes in oil, oil reserved

8 small slices Serrano or Iberico ham

5 black olives, pitted and sliced

1 small bunch chives, half chopped, half cut into short lengths

1. Arrange the baguette slices on a serving plate and spread each one with goat's cheese.
2. Put the sundried tomatoes and their oil in a mini food processor and blend to a loose paste.
3. Spoon some of the paste on top of each baguette slice and arrange a slice of ham on top of each one.
4. Garnish with olives, chopped chives and a few short lengths of chive.

MAKES: **8** | PREP TIME: **10 MINS**

Tomato and Black Pepper Montaditos

8 slices baguette

½ clove of garlic

4 ripe tomatoes, peeled, deseeded and chopped

1 shallot, quartered and thinly sliced

2 tbsp olive oil

½ tsp cracked black peppercorns

12 basil leaves

1. Arrange the baguette slices on a serving plate and rub it all over with the cut side of the garlic.

2. Mix the tomatoes with the shallot, oil and cracked pepper and season to taste with salt.

3. Spoon the tomatoes onto the baguette slices and serve immediately, garnished with basil.

Bread with Oil and Vinegar

75 ml / 2 ½ fl. oz / ⅓ cup olive oil
1 tbsp Pedro Ximenez balsamic vinegar
1 baguette
mixed olives, to serve

1. Pour the oil into a shallow serving dish and drizzle the vinegar over the top.
2. Tear the baguette into bite-sized pieces just before serving and arrange on a platter.
3. Add the oil dish and serve with mixed olives on the side.

Mini Vegetable Empanadillas

50 g / 1 ¾ oz / ¼ cup butter, cubed and chilled
125 g / 4 ½ oz / ¾ cup plain (all-purpose) flour
50 ml / 1 ¾ fl. oz / ¼ cup dry white wine
2 tbsp olive oil
1 onion, finely chopped
1 carrot, finely chopped
2 cloves of garlic, crushed
½ tsp ground cumin
150 g / 5 ½ oz / 1 cup peas, defrosted if frozen
1 medium potato, peeled and diced
250 ml / 9 fl. oz / 1 cup vegetable stock
sunflower oil, for deep frying
shredded spring onion (scallions), to serve

1. Rub the butter into the flour until the mixture resembles fine breadcrumbs. Stir in the wine and bring the pastry together into a pliable dough, adding a little water if needed. Chill for 1 hour.
2. Meanwhile, heat the oil in a large saucepan and fry the onion and carrot for 10 minutes, stirring occasionally. Add the garlic and cumin and cook for 2 minutes, then add the peas and potatoes. Pour in the stock and simmer for 20 minutes, then season to taste with salt and pepper. Leave to cool completely.
3. Roll out the pastry on a lightly floured surface and cut it into 16 squares. Drain the filling of any excess liquid, then spoon it onto one half of each square.
4. Brush around the edge with water then fold the pastries in half and press the edges firmly to seal.
5. Heat the sunflower oil in a deep fat fryer to a temperature of 180°C (350F). Fry the empanadillas in batches for 3 minutes, turning them when they float to the top.
6. Drain well on kitchen paper, then serve, garnished with spring onion.

Hake Goujons

800 g / 1 lb 12 oz / 5 ⅓ cups skinless
  boneless hake
50 g / 1 ¾ oz / ⅓ cup plain
  (all-purpose) flour
2 eggs, beaten
150 g / 5 ½ oz / 1 cup fine
  dried breadcrumbs
sunflower oil, for deep frying

1. Cut the hake into 18 evenly sized goujons. Put the flour, egg and panko breadcrumbs in three separate bowls.
2. Dip the hake first in the flour, then in the egg, then in the breadcrumbs.
3. Heat the oil in a deep fat fryer, according to the manufacturer's instructions, to a temperature of 180°C (350F).
4. Lower the fish fingers in the fryer basket and cook for 4 minutes or until crisp and golden brown. You may need to cook them in two batches to avoid overcrowding the fryer, in which case keep the first batch warm in a low oven.
5. Line a large bowl with a few layers of kitchen paper and when they are ready, tip them into the bowl to remove any excess oil.
6. Sprinkle with a little sea salt to taste and serve immediately.

Salmon, Tomato and Mozzarella Montaditos

6 slices baguette
6 slices tomato, similar in diameter
  to the bread
6 slices mozzarella
½ tsp dried oregano
3 slices smoked salmon, halved
6 sprigs parsley

1. Arrange the baguette slices on a serving plate.
2. Top the baguette with the tomato and mozzarella and sprinkle with oregano.
3. Roll the halved smoked salmon sliced into a spiral and position on top of the mozzarella.
4. Garnish with parsley and serve immediately.

Plato de Aperitivo

6 slices Manchego cheese
6 slices Serrano or Iberico ham
6 walnuts, partially opened
100 g / 3 ½ oz / ⅔ cup black olives, pitted
fresh thyme, to garnish
crusty bread, to serve

1. Arrange the cheese, ham and walnuts on a serving plate.
2. Decant the olives into a bowl.
3. Garnish the plates with fresh thyme sprigs and serve with crusty bread.

MAKES: 6 | PREP TIME: 5 MINS | COOKING TIME: 3 MINS

Mascarpone Montaditos

6 slices rustic baguette
150 g / 5 ½ oz / ⅔ cup mascarpone
2 salted anchovy fillets
2 slices Serrano ham
2 tbsp roasted red peppers in oil, drained
micro salad leaves, to garnish

1. Toast the baguette slices under a hot grill and arrange on a serving plate.
2. Spread each slice generously with mascarpone.
3. Top two of the slices with anchovy filets and top two of the slices with ham.
4. Top the last two slices with roasted peppers.
5. Garnish with micro salad leaves and serve.

MAKES: **12** | PREP TIME: **5 MINS**

Goat's Cheese and Quail Egg Montaditos

12 slices seeded rye baguette
175 g / 6 oz / ¾ cup soft goat's cheese
6 hard-boiled quail eggs, halved
1 stick celery, sliced
micro salad leaves, to garnish

1. Arrange the baguette slices on a serving plate and spread each one with goat's cheese.
2. Top each slice with half a quail's egg, two slices of celery and garnish with micro salad leaves.
3. Sprinkle with salt and pepper and serve immediately.

Ham and Tomato Montaditos

100 g / 3 ½ oz / ⅔ cup Iberico ham
10 slices crusty baguette
½ clove of garlic
2 tbsp olive oil
1 ripe tomato, halved

1. Remove the ham from the fridge 20 minutes before serving.
2. Rub the baguette slices with the cut side of the garlic and drizzle with oil.
3. Rub them with the cut sides of the tomato, then top with ham and serve immediately.

Onion Rings

2 medium onions, peeled
300 ml / 10 ½ fl. oz / 1 ¼ cups milk
150 g / 3 ½ oz / 1 cup plain
   (all-purpose) flour
2 large eggs, beaten
150 g / 5 ½ oz / 1 cup fine
   dried breadcrumbs

1. Thickly slice the onions, then separate the slices into rings. Soak the onion rings in milk for 30 minutes, then carefully remove the inner membrane from each ring. Drain well and pat dry with kitchen paper.
2. Heat the oil in a deep fat fryer, according to the manufacturer's instructions, to a temperature of 180°C (350F).
3. Coat the onion rings in flour and shake off any excess. Dip them in egg, then roll in breadcrumbs to coat.
4. Fry the onion rings in batches for 3 minutes or until crisp and brown, then drain well and tip them into a kitchen paper lined bowl.
5. Serve immediately.

Boquerones en Vinaigre

450 g / 1 lb / 3 cups very fresh anchovies, gutted and heads removed
500 ml / 17 ½ fl. oz / 2 cups white wine vinegar
1 red onion, sliced
2 cloves of garlic, sliced
a few sprigs flat-leaf parsley
125 ml / 4 ½ fl. oz / ½ cup olive oil
bread and spring onion (scallion) tops, to serve

1. Put the anchovies in a glass or ceramic bowl and season with salt.
2. Pour over the vinegar and leave to marinate in the fridge for 6 hours.
3. Drain off the vinegar and sprinkle over the onion, garlic and parsley.
4. Pour over the oil and return to the fridge to marinate for 2 hours.
5. Discard the flavourings before serving on small slices of bread, sprinkled with spring onion greens.

SERVES: **6** | PREP TIME: **20 MINS** | COOKING TIME: **2 MINS**

Breaded Calamares

sunflower oil, for deep frying
50 g / 1 ¾ oz / ⅓ cup plain (all-purpose) flour
2 eggs, beaten
150 g / 5 ½ oz / 1 cup fine dried breadcrumbs
300 g / 10 ½ oz / 2 cups squid tubes, cleaned and sliced into rings
1 spring onion (scallion), thinly shredded
lemon wedges and romesco sauce, to serve

1. Heat the oil in a deep fat fryer, according to the manufacturer's instructions, to a temperature of 180°C (350F).
2. Put the flour, egg and breadcrumbs in three separate bowls. Working in small batches, dip the squid rings in the flour with one hand and shake off any excess.
3. Dip them in the egg with the other hand, then toss them into the breadcrumbs and use your floured hand to ensure they are thoroughly covered.
4. Fry the calamares in batches for 2 minutes or until golden brown.
5. Transfer the calamares to a kitchen paper lined bowl to blot away any excess oil, then transfer to a serving bowl and garnish with spring onions and lemon wedges. Serve immediately with romesco sauce.

MAKES: 8 | PREP TIME: 20 MINS | COOKING TIME: 15 MINS

Baked Stuffed Clams

100 ml / 3 ½ fl. oz / ½ cup dry white wine
12 large live fresh clams, scrubbed
2 tbsp olive oil
1 shallot, finely chopped
1 clove of garlic, crushed
75 g / 2 ½ oz / 1 cup fresh
  white breadcrumbs
½ lemon, juiced and zest finely grated
25 g / 1 oz / ¼ cup Manchego, grated
1 tsp smoked paprika
2 tbsp parsley, finely chopped
lemon wedges, to serve

1. Preheat the oven to 180°C (160°C fan) / 350F / gas 4.
2. Put the wine in a saucepan and set it over a high heat. When it starts to boil, add the clams, then cover and steam for 4 minutes or until they have all opened.
3. Drain the clams, reserving the cooking liquor. Shell the clams, reserving eight half-shells, and chop the meat.
4. Heat the oil in a frying pan and fry the shallot and garlic for 5 minutes, without colouring. Take the pan off the heat and stir in the breadcrumbs, lemon zest and juice, Manchego, clams and enough of the clam cooking liquor to make a stiff paste.
5. Roll the mixture into eight balls and press each one into a clam shell. Arrange the clams in a baking dish and sprinkle the tops with paprika.
6. Bake for 15 minutes or until golden brown. Sprinkle with parsley and serve immediately with lemon wedges for squeezing over.

MAKES: 6 | PREP TIME: 35 MINS | COOKING TIME: 5 MINS

Lamb Triangles

2 tbsp olive oil

1 small onion, finely chopped

1 medium potato, finely diced

2 cloves of garlic, crushed

250 g / 9 oz / 1 cup minced lamb

¼ tsp hot paprika

½ tsp ground cumin

½ tsp ground coriander

50 g / 1 ¾ oz / ⅓ cup frozen peas, defrosted

6 sheets filo or brik pastry

100 g / 3 ½ oz / ½ cup butter, melted

sunflower oil, for deep-frying

1. Heat the olive oil in a frying pan and fry the onion for 5 minutes. Add the potatoes and sauté for 5 minutes.
2. Add the garlic and minced lamb cook for 5 more minutes then add the spices and peas. Turn off the heat and leave to cool.
3. Brush each pastry sheet with melted butter and fold it in half lengthways. Brush them with butter again.
4. Arrange a large spoonful of the filling at the end of one of the sheets, then fold the corner over and triangle-fold it up. Repeat with the rest of the pastry and filling to make six pastries.
5. Heat the oil in a deep fat fryer, according to the manufacturer's instructions, to a temperature of 180°C (350F).
6. Deep fry the pastries for 5 minutes or until golden brown and crisp. Drain on kitchen paper and serve hot.

Gambas Pil Pil

50 ml / 1 ¾ fl. oz / ¼ cup olive oil
2 hot red chillies (chilies), sliced
20 raw king prawns
1 tsp smoked paprika
1 tsp sea salt flakes
1 handful basil leaves
1 lemon, cut into wedges

1. Heat the oil in a large sauté pan over a high heat and fry the chilli for 1 minute 30 seconds.
2. Add the prawns and stir-fry until they turn opaque all over.
3. Sprinkle over the paprika and salt and stir-fry for 1 more minute.
4. Tip the prawns onto a serving plate and garnish with basil and lemon wedges.

Avocado Montaditos

3 ripe avocados, peeled, stoned and diced
½ lemon, juiced
½ red onion, finely chopped
½ red romano pepper, sliced
75 ml / 2 ½ fl. oz / ⅓ cup mayonnaise
2 tbsp mint leaves, roughly chopped, plus extra to garnish
8 slices rustic bread

1. Put the avocado in a bowl and douse it with lemon juice to stop it from discolouring.
2. Stir in the onion, pepper, mayonnaise and mint leaves and season well with salt and pepper.
3. Toast the bread under a hot grill until golden, then pile the avocado mixture on top.
4. Serve immediately.

SERVES: 6 | PREP TIME: 20 MINS | COOKING TIME: 25 MINS

Chorizo Sausage Rolls

450 g / 1 lb all-butter puff pastry

350 g / 12 oz cooking chorizo sausages

1 egg, beaten

1. Preheat the oven 230°C (210°C fan) / 450F / gas 8.
2. Roll out the pastry on a lightly floured surface into a large rectangle and cut it in half lengthways.
3. Arrange the sausages in a line down the length of the pastry strips and brush along the edges with beaten egg. Roll the sausages up in the pastry and press along the join firmly to seal.
4. Cut the rolls into bite sized pieces, score a cross in the top of each one and transfer to a baking tray.
5. Brush the tops with beaten egg and bake for 25 minutes or until golden brown and cooked through.

Gambas al Limon

12 raw king prawns, unpeeled
2 tbsp olive oil
½ lemon, sliced
1 clove of garlic, sliced
½ tsp ground coriander
mint sprigs, to serve

1. Put the prawns in a freezer bag with the oil, lemon, garlic and ground coriander. Seal and marinate in the fridge for 2 hours.
2. Heat a griddle pan until smoking hot. Tip the contents of the freezer bag into the pan and quickly spread it out into a single layer.
3. Fry the prawns for 2 minutes or until pink and opaque underneath.
4. Turn the prawns over and cook for another 2 minutes. They are ready when they have turned pink and opaque throughout.
5. Serve immediately, garnished with mint.

Olive and Sundried Tomato Montaditos

100 g / 3 ½ oz / ⅔ cup kalamata
  olives, pitted
100 g / 3 ½ oz / ⅔ cup green olives, pitted
100 g / 3 ½ oz / ½ cup sundried
  tomatoes in oil
1 shallot, finely chopped
½ clove of garlic, crushed
1 tbsp lemon juice
6 slices white bloomer

1. Put the olives and tomatoes on a large chopping board and chop them together with a big knife until well mixed.
2. Transfer to a bowl and stir in the shallot, garlic and lemon juice.
3. Spread the bread with the olive mixture and serve immediately.

SERVES: 4 | PREP TIME: 10 MINS | COOKING TIME: 30 MINS

Tortilla Espanol

50 ml / 1 ¾ fl. oz / ¼ cup olive oil
1 large onion, quartered and thinly sliced
4 boiled potatoes, cooled and cubed
6 large eggs

1. Heat half the oil in a non-stick frying pan and fry the onion with a pinch of salt and pepper for 10 minutes. Add the potatoes and cook for 5 minutes.

2. Meanwhile, gently beat the eggs in a jug to break up the yolks. When the vegetables are ready, stir them into the eggs and season with salt and pepper.

3. Heat the rest of the oil in the frying pan then pour in the egg mixture. Cook over a gentle heat for 8 minutes or until the egg has set around the outside, but the centre is still a bit runny.

4. Slide it onto a plate, then flip it over back into the pan. Cook the other side for 4 minutes or until cooked to your liking.

5. Leave to cool for 5 minutes before serving.

MAKES: **24** | PREP TIME: **2 HOURS 30 MINS** | COOKING TIME: **12 MINS**

Cheese and Sesame Breadsticks

400 g / 14 oz / 2 ⅔ cups strong white bread flour, plus extra for dusting
½ tsp easy blend dried yeast
1 tsp fine sea salt
1 tbsp olive oil
1 egg, beaten
100 g / 3 ½ oz / 1 cup Manchego, grated
2 tbsp mixed black and white sesame seeds

1. Mix together the flour, yeast and salt. Stir the oil into 280 ml of warm water then stir it into the dry ingredients.
2. Knead the mixture on a lightly oiled surface for 10 minutes or until smooth and elastic.
3. Leave the dough to rest in a lightly oiled bowl, covered with oiled clingfilm, for 1–2 hours or until doubled in size.
4. Preheat the oven to 220°C (200°C fan) / 425F / gas 7.
5. Roll out the dough into a large rectangle and cut it into 24 thin strips.
6. Transfer the breadsticks to two greased baking trays and leave to prove for 15 minutes.
7. Brush the breadsticks with egg and sprinkle with cheese and sesame seeds.
8. Bake for 12 minutes or until crisp. Transfer to a wire rack and leave to cool a little before serving warm.

SERVES: 6 | PREP TIME: 10 MINS

Cecina and Manchego Montaditos

6 slices rustic bread
100 g / 3 ½ oz / ½ cup cream cheese
6 thin slices Manchego, rind removed
6 lettuce leaves
12 slices cecina (cured beef)

1. Arrange the bread on a serving board and spread with cream cheese.
2. Top with Manchego and lettuce.
3. Arrange two slices of cecina on top of each one and serve immediately.

Battered Boquerones

sunflower oil, for deep frying

200 g / 7 oz / 1 ⅓ cups plain
  (all purpose) flour

1 tsp smoked paprika

2 tbsp olive oil

250 ml / 9 fl. oz / 1 cup sparkling water,
  well chilled

450 g / 1 lb / 3 cups fresh
  anchovies, gutted

1 tbsp sesame seeds

lettuce leaves and lemon wedges,
  to garnish

1. Heat the oil in a deep fat fryer, according to the manufacturer's instructions, to a temperature of 180°C (350F).
2. Sieve the flour and paprika into a bowl then whisk in the oil and water until smoothly combined. Dip the anchovies in the batter and fry in batches for 6 minutes or until golden brown and crisp.
3. Transfer the anchovies to a kitchen paper lined bowl to remove any excess oil.
4. Sprinkle the anchovies with salt and sesame seeds and serve on lettuce leaf lined plates with lemon wedges for squeezing over.

Barbecued Banana Peppers

4 sweet banana peppers

2 tbsp olive oil

1. Brush the peppers with oil.
2. Cook over prepared barbecue coals or in a hot griddle pan for 8 minutes, turning regularly.
3. Sprinkle with salt and serve hot or at room temperature.

Cream Cheese and Prawn Montaditos

10 slices baguette
150 g / 5 ½ oz / ⅔ cup cream cheese
10 lamb's lettuce leaves
20 short lengths spring onion (scallion) greens
10 cooked prawns (shrimp), peeled

1. Arrange the baguette slices on a serving plate and spread with cream cheese.
2. Place a lamb's lettuce leaf and two short lengths of spring onion greens on top of each one.
3. Top with the prawns and serve immediately.

MAKES: 8 | PREP TIME: 1 HOUR | CHILL TIME: 1 HOUR | COOKING TIME: 4 MINS

Beef and Rosemary Empanadillas

50 g / 1 ¾ oz / ¼ cup butter, cubed and chilled

125 g / 4 ½ oz / ¾ cup plain (all-purpose) flour

50 ml / 1 ¾ fl. oz / ¼ cup dry white wine

2 tbsp olive oil

1 onion, finely chopped

1 red pepper, diced

2 sprigs rosemary, leaves finely chopped, plus extra to garnish

1 red chilli (chili), finely chopped

2 cloves of garlic, crushed

1 tsp smoked paprika

225 g / 8 oz / 1 cup minced beef

200 ml / 7 fl. oz / ¾ cup beef stock

sunflower oil, for deep frying

1. Rub the butter into the flour until the mixture resembles breadcrumbs.
2. Stir in the wine and bring the pastry together into a pliable dough, adding a little water if needed. Chill for 1 hour.
3. Meanwhile, heat the oil in a large saucepan and fry the onion, pepper, rosemary and chilli for 3 minutes. Add the garlic and paprika and cook for 2 minutes, then add the mince.
4. Fry the mince until it starts to brown then add the stock and simmer for 20 minutes. Leave to cool completely.
5. Roll out the pastry on a lightly floured surface. Cut out eight circles with a 12 cm (5 in) round cookie cutter.
6. Drain the filling of any excess liquid, then spoon it onto the pastry circles.
7. Bush round the edge with water then fold the pastries in half and press the edges firmly to seal. Dimple round the edge with your finger.
8. Heat the sunflower oil in a deep fat fryer to a temperature of 180°C (350F). Fry the empanadillas in batches for 4 minutes, turning them when they float to the top.
9. Drain well on kitchen paper, then serve, garnished with extra rosemary.

MAKES: 12 | PREP TIME: 45 MIN | CHILL: 2 HOURS | COOKING TIME: 3 MINS

Cheese and Herb Croquetas

50 g / 1 ¾ oz / ¼ cup butter

½ leek, finely chopped

½ tsp dried oregano

1 tsp fresh rosemary, finely chopped

50 g / 1 ¾ oz / ⅓ cup plain
  (all-purpose) flour

450 ml / 16 fl. oz / 1 ¾ cups whole milk

75 g / 2 ½ oz / ¾ cup Manchego, grated

1 tbsp parsley, finely chopped

2 large eggs, beaten

150 g / 5 ½ oz / 1 cup fine
  dried breadcrumbs

sunflower oil, for deep frying

aioli to serve

1. Heat the butter in a saucepan and fry the leek, oregano and rosemary over a low heat for 10 minutes. Add the flour and stir over a low heat for 5 minutes, being carefully not to brown it too much.

2. Gradually whisk in the milk, then stir over a medium heat for 12 minutes or until it resembles soft mashed potato. Beat in the cheese and parsley, then spoon it into a piping bag fitted with a large plain nozzle and leave to cool completely. Chill for 2 hours.

3. Heat the oil in a deep fat fryer, according to the manufacturer's instructions, to a temperature of 180°C (350F).

4. Pipe 10 cm (4 in) lengths of the mixture into the beaten egg and turn to coat. Transfer them to a bowl of breadcrumbs and turn to coat thoroughly.

5. Deep fry the croquetas in batches for 3 minutes or until golden and crisp.

6. Transfer the croquetas to a kitchen paper lined bowl to blot away any excess oil, then serve immediately with aioli.

MAKES: **6** | PREP TIME: **5 MINS**

Cheese, Ham and Olive Toasts

6 round toasts
½ clove of garlic
6 slices Canarejal or Camembert cheese
6 slices Serrano ham
6 green olives, pitted

1. Rub the top of each toast with the cut side of the garlic and arrange on a serving plate.
2. Spread a slice of Canarejal onto each one.
3. Top the cheese with a slice of ham and an olive.

MAKES: **12** | PREP TIME: **5 MINS** | COOKING TIME: **5 MINS**

Pan con Tomate

12 slices crusty baguette
1 clove of garlic, halved
2 tbsp olive oil
1 large ripe tomato, halved

1. Lightly toast the baguette slices under a hot grill.
2. Rub the toast with the cut side of the garlic and drizzle with oil.
3. Rub each piece with the cut sides of the tomato, then season with a little salt and pepper. Serve immediately.

MAKES: 8 | PREP TIME: 5 MINS | COOKING TIME: 4 MINS

Asparagus and Lomo Montaditos

150 g / 5 ½ oz thin asparagus spears, woody ends snapped off

50 ml / 1 ¾ fl. oz / ¼ cup olive oil

8 slices rustic baguette

8 slices lomo de bellota, torn into pieces

1. Brush the asparagus with half of the oil and season with salt and pepper. Cook the asparagus in a hot frying pan for 4 minutes, shaking the pan occasionally.

2. Meanwhile, toast the baguette slices under a hot grill and arrange on a serving plate.

3. Drizzle the toast with the rest of the oil, then arrange the asparagus and lomo on top.

MAKES: 6 | PREP TIME: 5 MINS

Goat's Cheese and Tomato Montaditos

6 slices square white sandwich loaf
100 g / 3 ½ oz / ½ cup soft goat's cheese
9 cherry tomatoes, quartered
1 handful baby spinach leaves
a few sprigs of dill

1. Spread the bread with goat's cheese and arrange on a serving plate.
2. Top with cherry tomatoes.
3. Garnish with spinach and dill and sprinkle with salt, then serve immediately.

MAKES: **10** | PREP TIME: **5 MINS** | COOKING TIME: **4 MINS**

Cream Cheese and Jalapeno Jelly Montaditos

12 slices baguette
150 g / 5 ½ oz / ⅔ cup cream cheese
125 g / 4 ½ oz / ⅓ cup jalapeno jelly

1. Toast the bread under a hot grill for a few minutes on each side until golden brown.
2. Leave to cool, then spread with cream cheese.
3. Spoon the jalapeno jelly on top and serve immediately.

Cazuelas
(Small Dishes of Tapas)

SERVES: **4** | PREP TIME: **15 MINS**

Mojo Rojo and Mojo Verde

FOR THE MOJO ROJO

1 red pepper, deseeded and chopped
1 red chilli (chili), chopped
1 tsp smoked paprika
¼ tsp ground cumin
2 tbsp sherry vinegar
75 ml / 2 ½ fl. oz / ⅓ cup olive oil

FOR THE MOJO VERDE

1 small green pepper, deseeded
  and chopped
1 small bunch fresh coriander (cilantro),
  chopped
2 cloves of garlic, crushed
¼ tsp ground cumin
2 tbsp sherry vinegar
75 ml / 2 ½ fl. oz / ⅓ cup olive oil

1. To make the Mojo Rojo, put the pepper, chilli, paprika, cumin and vinegar in a liquidizer with a big pinch of salt and blend to a thick paste.
2. Slowly add the olive oil with the motor still running and blend until smooth. Taste and adjust the seasoning.
3. To make the Mojo Verde, put the pepper, coriander, garlic, cumin and vinegar in a liquidizer with a big pinch of salt and blend to a thick paste.
4. Slowly add the olive oil with the motor still running and blend until smooth. Taste and adjust the seasoning.
5. Serve the sauces with papas arrugadas (see Pinchos chapter).

Albondigas

50 ml / 1 ¾ fl. oz / ¼ cup olive oil
1 onion, finely chopped
1 clove of garlic, crushed
250 g / 9 oz / 1 ⅔ cups minced beef
250 g / 9 oz / 1 ⅔ cups sausagemeat
50 g / 1 ¾ oz / ⅔ cup fresh
  white breadcrumbs
¼ tsp nutmeg, freshly grated
1 egg yolk
600 ml / 1 pint / 2 ½ cups tomato passata
flat leaf parsley, to garnish

1. Heat half of the oil in a large sauté pan and fry the onion for 8 minutes or until softened.
2. Add the garlic and cook for 2 more minutes, stirring constantly, then scrape the mixture into a mixing bowl and leave to cool.
3. Add the mince, sausagemeat, breadcrumbs, nutmeg and egg yolk and mix well, then shape into golf ball-sized meatballs.
4. Heat the rest of the oil in the sauté pan and sear the meatballs on all sides, then season with salt and pepper.
5. Pour over the passata, then cover and simmer for 15 minutes or until the meatballs are cooked through.
6. Garnish the meatballs with parsley and serve immediately.

Rice and Mung Bean Stew

125 g / 4 ½ oz / ⅔ cup moong dal (split
  mung beans)
50 g / 1 ¾ oz / ¼ cup whole dried
  mung beans
200 g / 7 oz / 1 cup paella rice, soaked
  for 1 hour
1 tsp ground cumin
1 tsp ground coriander
3 tbsp olive oil
2 cloves of garlic, finely chopped
2 bay leaves
1 tsp dried oregano

1. Toast the moong dal and mung beans in a dry frying pan over a medium heat for 3 minutes.
2. Heat 750 ml of water in a saucepan. When it starts to boil, stir in the rice, toasted dal and beans and spices. Boil for 12 minutes.
3. Heat the olive oil in a small frying pan and fry the garlic and bay leaves for 2 minutes. Stir the mixture into the rice pan and boil for another 18 minutes or until the rice and lentils are tender and the water has reduced to a porridge consistency.
4. Season to taste with salt and pepper, then sprinkle with oregano.

Salt Cod and Chickpea Stew

75 ml / 2 ½ fl. oz / ⅓ cup olive oil
1 onion, finely chopped
2 yellow peppers, deseeded and diced
3 cloves of garlic, finely chopped
1 tsp ground cumin
1 tsp smoked paprika
400 g / 14 oz / 2 cups canned chickpeas
   (garbanzo beans), drained
200 g / 7 oz / 1 cup canned
   tomatoes, chopped
300 g / 10 ½ oz / 2 cups salt cod, soaked
   for 24 hours, cut into chunks
1 handful raisins
flat leaf parsley, to garnish

1. Heat the oil in a large saucepan and fry the onion and peppers over a low heat for 18 minutes, stirring occasionally. Add the garlic and spices and stir-fry for 2 minutes.
2. Stir in the chickpeas and tomatoes, then add the cod and raisins.
3. Pour in just enough boiling water to cover the ingredients and simmer for 20 minutes or until the salt cod is tender.
4. Taste the sauce and adjust the seasoning, then serve garnished with parsley.

Gambas al Ajillo

50 ml / 1 ¾ fl. oz / ¼ cup olive oil
3 cloves of garlic, finely chopped
2 dried red chillies (chilies), sliced
36 raw king prawns, peeled with tails
   left intact
2 tbsp flat leaf parsley, finely chopped,
   plus a few sprigs to garnish
¼ tsp smoked paprika
½ lemon, juiced
toasted baguette slices, to serve

1. Heat the oil in a large sauté pan over a high heat and fry the garlic and chilli for 1 minute 30 seconds.
2. Add the prawns and stir-fry until they start to turn pink in places.
3. Add the chopped parsley and paprika and continue to stir-fry until the prawns are pink all over.
4. Season with salt and add lemon juice to taste, then divide the prawns between four warm bowls. Garnish with parsley and serve with toasted baguette slices on the side.

SERVES: **2** | PREP TIME: **5 MINS** | COOKING TIME: **15 MINS**

Fried Eggs with Potatoes

3 medium potatoes, peeled and diced
75 ml /2 ½ fl. oz / ⅓ cup olive oil
2 cloves of garlic, thinly sliced
2 red chillies (chilies), sliced
100 g 3 ½ oz / ¾ cup cooked leftover vegetables, eg. asparagus, chopped
4 small eggs
1 pinch saffron
1 tbsp parsley, finely chopped
garlic bread, to serve

1. Parboil the potatoes in salted water for 4 minutes, then drain well and dry with a clean tea towel.
2. Heat 50 ml of the oil in a large sauté pan and add the potatoes. Fry over a medium heat for 5 minutes without disturbing them.
3. Add the garlic, chillies and vegetables to the pan and sauté for 5 minutes or until the potatoes are golden brown.
4. Meanwhile, heat the rest of the oil in a frying pan and break in the eggs. Sprinkle with saffron and fry for 3 minutes, basting regularly with oil from the pan.
5. Season the potatoes and eggs with plenty of salt and pepper, then spoon them into two terracotta dishes. Sprinkle with parsley and serve immediately with garlic bread.

SERVES: **4** | PREP TIME: **35 MINS** | COOKING TIME: **20 MINS**

Chicken and Pork Albondigas

50 ml / 1 ¾ fl. oz / ¼ cup olive oil

2 onions, finely chopped

2 cloves of garlic, crushed

200 g / 7 oz / 1 cup canned tomatoes, chopped

½ tsp smoked paprika

250 g / 9 oz / 1 ⅔ cups minced chicken

250 g / 9 oz / 1 ⅔ cups sausagemeat

50 g / 1 ¾ oz / ⅔ cup fresh white breadcrumbs

2 tsp fresh thyme leaves, finely chopped

1 egg yolk

1. Heat half of the oil in a large sauté pan and fry the onion for 8 minutes or until softened.
2. Add the garlic and cook for 2 more minutes, stirring constantly, then scrape half of the mixture into a mixing bowl and leave to cool.
3. Add the tomatoes and paprika to the sauté pan and simmer for 10 minutes.
4. Meanwhile, add the chicken, sausagemeat, breadcrumbs, thyme and egg yolk to the onion bowl and mix well. Season with salt and pepper, then shape into eight meatballs.
5. Heat the rest of the oil in a frying pan and cook the meatballs over a medium-low heat for 18 minutes, turning regularly.
6. Add the tomato sauce to the pan and simmer for 2 more minutes, then serve.

SERVES: **6** | PREP TIME: **5 MINS** | COOKING TIME: **15 MINS**

Guindillas with Garlic and Dill

250 g / 9 oz / 3 ⅓ cups Guindillas Verde
50 ml / 1 ¾ fl. oz / ¼ cup olive oil
1 clove of garlic, thinly sliced
2 tbsp fresh dill, finely chopped

1. Preheat the oven to 220°C (200°C fan) / 425F / gas 7.
2. Toss the Guindillas with half of the oil and spread them out in a roasting tin. Roast for 15 minutes or until softened and browned, turning halfway through.
3. Fry the garlic gently in the rest of the oil for 1 minute, then toss with the Guindillas and dill.
4. Season with salt and pepper and serve immediately.

Fried Potatoes

4 large floury potatoes, peeled and cut
into chunks

sunflower oil, for deep frying

1. Heat the oil in a deep fat fryer, according to the manufacturer's instructions, to a temperature of 130°C (265F).
2. Put the potatoes in the fryer basket and cook for 15 minutes so that they cook through but don't brown. You may need to do this in batches so that the fryer is not overcrowded.
3. Pull up the fryer basket then increase the fryer temperature to 190°C (375F). When the oil has come up to temperature, lower the fryer basket and cook the potatoes for 5 minutes or until crisp and golden brown.
4. Line a large bowl with a few layers of kitchen paper and when the potatoes are ready, tip them into the bowl to remove any excess oil.
5. Serve with cocktail sticks to make it easier for dipping.

Pumpkin Rice

50 ml / 1 ¾ fl. oz / ¼ cup olive oil

1 onion, finely chopped

300 g / 10 ½ oz / 2 cups pumpkin or
butternut squash, diced

2 cloves of garlic, crushed

250 g / 9 oz / 1 ¼ cups paella rice

50 g / 1 ¾ oz Manchego, finely grated

¼ tsp nutmeg, freshly grated

1. Preheat the oven to 180°C (160°C fan) / 350F / gas 4.
2. Heat the olive oil in a cast iron casserole dish and gently fry the onion and pumpkin for 10 minutes without colouring. Add the garlic and cook for 2 more minutes then add the rice and stir well to coat in the oil.
3. Add 500 ml of water and season with salt and pepper, then stir well.
4. Cover the dish and transfer to the oven to cook for 30 minutes, stirring every 10 minutes.
5. When the rice is tender and the pumpkin has broken down into a puree, beat in the Manchego and nutmeg with a wooden spoon.
6. Adjust the seasoning if necessary, then spoon into a serving dish.

SERVES: 4 | **PREP TIME: 5 MINS** | **MARINATE: 2 HOURS** | **COOKING TIME: 12 MINS**

Griddled Marinated Artichokes

8 baby artichokes, trimmed
  and quartered
1 lemon, juiced
75 ml / 2 ½ fl. oz / ⅓ cup olive oil
1 tsp dried oregano
2 cloves of garlic, crushed

1. Douse the artichokes liberally with lemon juice to prevent discolouration, then transfer them to a freezer bag and add the oil, oregano and garlic. Marinate in the fridge for 2 hours.

2. Preheat the oven to 190°C (170°C fan) / 375F / gas 5. and heat an oven-proof griddle pan on the hob until smoking hot.

3. Season the artichokes with salt and pepper, then griddle the first side for 4 minutes.

4. Turn the artichokes over, then transfer the griddle pan to the oven and roast for 8 minutes or until tender to the point of a knife.

5. Serve hot straight away or chill and serve cold.

SERVES: 4 | PREP TIME: 5 MINS | COOKING TIME: 40 MINS

Paella

1 litre / 1 pint 15 fl. oz / 4 cups
  chicken stock

a pinch of saffron

50 ml / 1 ¾ fl. oz / ¼ cup olive oil

1 onion, diced

1 red pepper, diced

2 cloves of garlic, crushed

100 g / 3 ½ oz / ⅔ cup frozen
  peas, defrosted

100 g / 3 ½ oz / ⅔ cup runner beans,
  cut into short lengths

200 g / 7 oz / 1 cup paella rice

6 raw king prawns

5 green-lip mussels, scrubbed

1 handful small clams, scrubbed

1. Heat the stock in a saucepan with the saffron, but don't let it boil.
2. Heat the olive oil in a paella pan and fry the onion and pepper for 15 minutes without colouring. Add the garlic and cook for 2 minutes.
3. Stir in the peas, beans and rice and season with salt and pepper. Stir well to coat with the oil, then pour in the hot stock and stir once more.
4. Simmer without stirring for 10 minutes or until there's only just enough stock left to cover the rice. Distribute the prawns, mussels and clams evenly across the surface and press them down into the liquid. Simmer without stirring for 5 more minutes.
5. Cover the pan with foil or a lid, turn off the heat and leave to stand for 5 minutes. Discard the upper half of the mussel shells.
6. Serve immediately.

SERVES: **4** | PREP TIME: **5 MINS** | COOKING TIME: **15 MINS**

Bulgur and Tomato Salad

350 ml / 12 ½ fl. oz / 1 ½ cups vegetable stock
150 g / 5 ½ oz / ¾ cup bulgur wheat
50 ml / 1 ¾ fl. oz / ¼ cup olive oil
1 clove of garlic, finely chopped
3 salted anchovy fillets, rinsed and chopped
1 lemon, juiced and zest finely grated
100 g / 3 ½ oz / ⅔ cup mixed yellow and red cherry tomatoes, chopped

1. Bring the vegetable stock to the boil in a small saucepan. Add the bulgur wheat, then cover, take the pan off the heat and leave to soak for 15 minutes.
2. Heat the oil in a sauté pan and fry the garlic and anchovy for 1 minute, then take the pan off the heat.
3. When the bulgur is ready, drain any excess stock and stir it into the anchovy pan with the lemon juice, zest and tomatoes.
4. Season to taste with salt and pepper and serve hot or cold.

SERVES: **6** | PREP TIME: **10 MINS** | MARINATING TIME: **2 HOURS**

Marinated Olives

2 red chillies (chilies), chopped
2 cloves of garlic, chopped
¼ roasted red pepper in oil, drained and chopped
150 g / 5 ½ oz / 1 cup mixed olives in brine, pitted and drained
a few sprigs flat leaf parsley, chopped

1. Pound the chillies with a pestle and mortar until well pulped, then add the garlic and pound again. Add the roasted pepper and grind to a paste.
2. Mix the olives with the pepper paste and chopped parsley.
3. Cover and leave to marinate for at least 2 hours before serving.

SERVES: 6 | **PREP TIME: 10 MINS** | **COOKING TIME: 1 HOUR 5 MINS**

Octopus with Fried Potatoes

2 bay leaves

1 lemon, zest finely pared with a vegetable peeler

1 garlic bulb, halved horizontally

1 tbsp sea salt

1 octopus, cleaned and defrosted if frozen

75 ml / 2 ½ fl. oz / ⅓ cup olive oil

1 large onion, halved and thinly sliced

2 cloves of garlic, sliced

4 large waxy potatoes, peeled and cubed

1 tsp smoked paprika

1 small bunch flat leaf parsley, thinly sliced

1. Bring a large saucepan of water to the boil and add the bay leaf, lemon zest, garlic and salt.

2. Submerge the octopus and simmer for 45 minutes.

3. Meanwhile, heat the oil in a large sauté pan and fry the onion for 15 minutes or until golden brown and sticky. Add the garlic and cook for 2 minutes, then transfer to a bowl with a slotted spoon. Save the oil in the sauté pan.

4. Add the potatoes to the octopus saucepan and simmer for a further 5 minutes, then drain well. Blot the potatoes dry with a clean tea towel.

5. Reheat the oil in the sauté pan and add the potatoes. Fry for 5 minutes without disturbing, then sauté for another 5 minutes.

6. Meanwhile, discard the eyes and beak of the octopus and cut the rest into bite-sized pieces. Add the octopus to the potato pan with the fried onions and sauté for 5 minutes. Season to taste with paprika, salt and pepper and serve sprinkled with parsley.

MAKES: 10 | PREP TIME: 45 MINS | CHILL: 1 HOUR | COOKING TIME: 4 MINS

Empanadillas

50 g / 1 ¾ oz / ¼ cup butter, cubed
and chilled

125 g / 4 ½ oz / ¾ cup plain
(all-purpose) flour

50 ml / 1 ¾ fl. oz / ¼ cup dry white wine

2 tbsp olive oil

1 onion, finely chopped

2 cloves of garlic, crushed

1 red chilli (chili), finely chopped

150 g / 5 ½ oz / 1 cup canned tuna,
drained and flaked

1 large tomato, peeled, deseeded
and chopped

½ lemon, juiced

2 tsp red pepper flakes

sunflower oil, for deep frying

a few sprigs rosemary

romesco sauce, to serve

1. Rub the butter into the flour until the
   mixture resembles fine breadcrumbs.
   Stir in the wine and bring the pastry
   together into a pliable dough,
   adding a little water if needed.
   Chill for 1 hour.

2. Heat the olive oil in a frying pan and
   fry the onion for 5 minutes, stirring
   occasionally. Add the garlic and chilli
   and cook for 2 minutes, then add
   the tuna, tomato and lemon juice.
   Cook for 3 minutes, then leave to
   cool completely.

3. Sprinkle the work surface with pepper
   flakes, then roll the pastry out on top.
   Cut out 10 circles with a 10 cm (4 in)
   fluted cookie cutter. Drain the filling
   of any excess liquid, then spoon it
   onto the pastry circles.

4. Brush around the edge with water
   then fold the pastries in half and press
   the edges firmly to seal.

5. Heat the sunflower oil in a deep
   fat fryer to a temperature of 180°C
   (350F). Fry the empanadillas in
   batches for 4 minutes, turning them
   when they float to the top.

6. Drain well on kitchen paper, then
   transfer to a bowl and garnish with
   rosemary. Serve immediately with
   romesco sauce for dipping.

Olives with Sundried Tomatoes and Herbs

100 g / 3 ½ oz / ⅔ cup green olives in brine, pitted and drained

100 g / 3 ½ oz / ⅔ cup kalamata olives in brine, drained

75 g / 2 ½ oz / ⅓ cup sundried tomatoes in oil, drained and chopped

a few sprigs fresh thyme

a few sprigs fresh rosemary

175 ml / 6 fl. oz / ⅔ cup olive oil

1. Mix the olives with the sundried tomatoes, thyme and rosemary and pack them tightly into sterilised glass jars.
2. Add enough olive oil to cover by 1 cm (½ in), then screw on the lids.
3. Leave the olives to marinate at room temperature for 1 week before serving.

Prawn and Chicken Paella

1 litre / 1 pint 15 fl. oz / 4 cups chicken stock

a pinch of saffron

50 ml / 1 ¾ fl. oz / ¼ cup olive oil

2 skinless boneless chicken thighs, diced

1 onion, sliced

2 orange peppers, sliced

2 cloves of garlic, sliced

100 g / 3 ½ oz / ⅔ cup frozen peas, defrosted

200 g / 7 oz / 1 cup paella rice

8 raw king prawns, peeled with tails left intact

lime wedges, to garnish

1. Heat the stock in a saucepan with the saffron, but don't let it boil.
2. Heat half the olive oil in a paella pan and brown the chicken all over. Transfer to a bowl with a slotted spoon. Add the rest of the oil to the pan and fry the onion and pepper for 15 minutes without colouring. Add the garlic and cook for 2 minutes.
3. Stir in the peas and rice and season with salt and pepper. Stir well to coat with the oil, then pour in the hot stock and stir once more.
4. Simmer without stirring for 10 minutes or until there's only just enough stock left to cover the rice. Distribute the prawns and chicken evenly across the surface and press them down into the liquid. Simmer without stirring for 5 more minutes.
5. Cover the pan with foil or a lid, turn off the heat and leave to stand for 5 minutes. Serve immediately, garnished with lime.

Chorizo

150 g / 5 ½ oz piece chorizo ring

1. Make a small incision into the skin at one end of the chorizo, then tear and remove the outer casing.
2. Cut the chorizo into 5 mm slices and arrange in a small serving bowl.
3. Allow the chorizo to come up to room temperature for at least 15 minutes for the best texture. Ideally, it should be served at 21°C (70F).

Gambas with Lemon, Garlic and Parsley

2 tbsp olive oil
1 clove of garlic, sliced
1 red chilli (chili), chopped
8 raw king prawns, unpeeled
2 slices lemon

1. Heat a sauté pan over a high heat and add the oil.
2. Add the garlic, chilli, prawns and lemon and stir-fry for 5 minutes or until the prawns have turned opaque all over.
3. Season with salt and pepper and serve immediately.

SERVES: 4 | PREP TIME: 5 MINS | COOKING TIME: 10 MINS

Setas al Ajillo

50 ml / 1 ¾ fl. oz / ¼ cup olive oil
3 cloves of garlic, finely chopped
200 g / 7 oz / 2 ⅔ cups mushrooms, sliced
2 tbsp flat leaf parsley, finely chopped

1. Heat the oil in a large sauté pan over a high heat and fry the garlic for 1 minute 30 seconds.
2. Add the mushrooms and sauté for 5 minutes.
3. Add the parsley and season with salt and pepper, then sauté for another 2 minutes. Spoon into a bowl and serve immediately.

Pinchos

(Tapas With a Utensil)

SERVES: **4** | PREP TIME: **30 MINS** | MARINATE: **30 MINS** | COOKING TIME: **4 MINS**

Prawn and Scallop Skewers

12 raw prawns, peeled with tails left intact
8 scallops, shelled
50 ml / 1 ¾ fl. oz / ¼ cup olive oil
1 clove of garlic, crushed
1 lemon, juiced and zest finely grated
½ tsp ground coriander
2 tbsp fresh coriander (cilantro),
  finely chopped

1. Soak four wooden skewers in cold water for 20 minutes.
2. Thread the prawns and scallops onto the skewers.
3. Mix the olive oil with the garlic, lemon zest and ground coriander and season with salt and pepper. Brush the mixture over the skewers and leave to marinate for 30 minutes.
4. Cook the skewers over a hot barbecue or in a smoking hot griddle pan for 2 minutes on each side or until the prawns and scallops are opaque in the centre and lightly charred on the outside.
5. Drizzle the skewers with lemon juice and serve scattered with chopped coriander.

MAKES: **16** | PREP TIME: **20 MINS** | MARINATING TIME: **2 WEEKS**

Cheese-stuffed Pickled Chillies

16 mild chillies, stalks and seeds removed
350 ml / 12 ½ fl. oz / 1 ½ cups white wine vinegar
100 g / 3 ½ oz / ½ cup cream cheese
50 g / 1 ¾ oz / ½ cup Manchego, finely grated
1 bay leaf
300 ml / 10 ½ fl. oz / 1 ¼ cups olive oil

1. Pack the chillies, open end up in a glass jar. Sprinkle with 1 tsp of salt, then pour over enough vinegar to cover the completely. Cover and leave at room temperature for 1 week.
2. Drain the chillies. The chilli-infused vinegar can be used in dressings or the next batch of pickles.
3. Mix the cream cheese with the Manchego and use the mixture to fill the chillies.
4. Pack the chillies back into the jar and tuck in the bay leaf. Fill the jar with olive oil, then cover and leave to stand at room temperature for 1 week before serving.

SERVES: 2 | PREP TIME: 10 MINS | COOKING TIME: 8 MINS

Fillet Steak with Herb Cheese

2 x 250 g / 9 oz fillet steaks
2 slices garlic and herb cheese, halved

1. Preheat the oven to 200°C (180°C fan) / 400F / gas 6 and put a griddle pan on to heat for 5 minutes or until smoking hot.
2. Dry the steaks really well with kitchen paper, then season liberally with sea salt and black pepper.
3. Transfer the steaks to the griddle pan and cook without disturbing for 3 minutes. Turn them over, then transfer the pan to the oven and roast for 5 minutes.
4. Transfer the steaks to a warm plate and top with the cheese. Cover with foil and leave to rest for 5 minutes before serving.

Stuffed Vine Leaves

12 vine leaves in brine
2 tbsp olive oil
1 small onion, finely chopped
1 clove of garlic, crushed
3 tomatoes, peeled deseeded and
    finely chopped
1 tsp tomato puree
250 g / 9 oz / 1 ½ cups cold cooked rice
½ lemon, juiced
2 tbsp flat leaf parsley, chopped
2 tbsp coriander (cilantro), chopped

1. Soak the vine leaves in boiling water for 20 minutes, then drain well and spread them out on a clean worksurface.
2. Meanwhile, heat the oil in a frying pan and fry the onion for 10 minutes. Add the garlic and cook for 2 minutes, then stir in the tomatoes and tomato puree. Cook for 3 minutes, then stir in the rice, lemon juice and herbs. Season to taste with salt and pepper.
3. Put a tablespoon of the rice mixture in the centre of the first leaf and roll up, tucking the sides in as you go. Repeat with the rest of the leaves and rice.
4. Pack the stuffed vine leaves into a saucepan and weigh them down with a plate. Pour in enough boiling water to cover by 2.5 cm (1 in) and add 1 teaspoon of salt, then cover the pan and simmer gently for 1 hour.
5. Serve hot or cold.

Salami Pinchos

6 slices baguette
2 tbsp olive oil
9 slices salchichon
9 slices salchicha Polaca
6 green olives, pitted
6 parsley leaves

1. Arrange the baguette slices on a serving board and drizzle with olive oil.
2. Skewer three salchichon slices onto each of three of the baguette slices with a cocktail stick. Skewer the salchicha Polaca slices onto the other three slices.
3. Thread an olive onto each cocktail stick and serve garnished with parsley.

Potatas Bravas

4 large floury potatoes, peeled and cut
 into chunks

sunflower oil, for deep frying

75 ml / 2 ½ fl. oz / ⅓ cup tomato ketchup

1 tsp smoked paprika

2 tbsp olive oil

1 clove garlic, crushed

2 tsp lemon juice

½ tsp dried oregano

½ tsp dried thyme

75 ml / 2 ½ fl. oz / ⅓ cup mayonnaise

1. Heat the oil in a deep fat fryer, according to the manufacturer's instructions, to a
   temperature of 130°C (265F).
2. Lower the potatoes in the fryer basket and cook for 15 minutes so that they cook all
   the way through but don't brown. You may need to do this in batches so that the
   fryer isn't overcrowded.
3. While the potatoes are cooking, stir the ketchup, smoked paprika and olive oil
   together to make a simple bravas sauce. Stir the garlic, lemon juice and herbs into
   the mayonnaise to make a simple herb aioli.
4. When the 15 minutes are up, pull up the fryer basket then increase the fryer
   temperature to 190°C (375F). When the oil has come up to temperature, lower the
   fryer basket and cook the potatoes for 5 minutes or until crisp and golden brown.
5. Line a large bowl with a few layers of kitchen paper and when the potatoes are
   ready, tip them into the bowl to remove any excess oil.
6. Transfer the potatoes to a serving bowl and serve immediately with the two sauces.

Pimentos de Padron

50 ml / 1 ¾ fl. oz / ¼ cup olive oil

250 g / 9 oz / 3 ⅓ cups pimentos
 de padron

1-2 tsp sea salt flakes

1. Heat the olive oil in a very large frying pan over a medium heat.
2. Fry the pimentos de padron for 5 minutes or until softened and blistered all over.
3. Transfer to a serving plate with a slotted spoon and season with sea salt flakes
   to taste.

MAKES: 16 | **PREP TIME: 40 MINS** | **CHILL: 2 HOURS** | **COOKING TIME: 3 MINS**

Ham Croquetas

50 g / 1 ¾ oz / ¼ cup butter
½ leek, finely chopped
3 thick slices Serrano ham, finely diced
50 g / 1 ¾ oz / ⅓ cup plain
  (all-purpose) flour
450 ml / 16 fl. oz / 1 ¾ cups whole milk
25 g / 1 oz / ¼ cup Manchego, grated
¼ tsp nutmeg, freshly grated
2 large eggs, beaten
150 g / 5 ½ oz / 1 cup fine dried breadcrumbs
sunflower oil, for deep frying

1. Heat the butter in a saucepan and fry the leek and ham over a low heat for
   5 minutes. Add the flour and stir over a low heat for 5 minutes, being carefully not
   to brown it too much.
2. Gradually whisk in the milk, then stir over a medium heat for 12 minutes or until it
   resembles soft mashed potato. Beat in the cheese and nutmeg, then leave to cool
   completely. Chill for 2 hours.
3. Heat the oil in a deep fat fryer, according to the manufacturer's instructions, to a
   temperature of 180°C (350F).
4. Scoop heaped teaspoons of the mixture into the beaten egg and turn to coat.
   Transfer them to a bowl of breadcrumbs and turn to coat thoroughly.
5. Deep fry the croquetas in batches for 3 minutes or until golden and crisp.
6. Transfer the croquetas to a kitchen paper lined bowl to blot away any excess oil,
   then serve immediately.

SERVES: 6 | PREP TIME: 45 MINS | CHILL: 2 HOURS | COOKING TIME: 5 MINS

Prawn and Salt Cod Fritters

500 ml / 17 ½ fl. oz / 2 cups whole milk

1 onion, peeled and halved

3 cloves of garlic, squashed

1 bay leaf

200 g / 7 oz / 1 ⅓ cups salt cod, soaked for 24 hours

250 g / 9 oz / 2 cups potatoes, peeled and cut into chunks

150 g / 5 ½ oz / 1 cup raw prawns (shrimp), peeled

1 small bunch parsley, chopped

1 small bunch coriander (cilantro), chopped

100 g / 3 ½ oz / ⅔ cup plain (all-purpose) flour

sunflower oil, for deep frying

1. Put the milk in a saucepan with the onion, garlic and bay leaf and bring to a gentle simmer. Lower in the salt cod and simmer for 5 minutes.

2. Strain the milk into a clean saucepan and add the potatoes. Cook for 12 minutes or until the potatoes are tender all the way through. Meanwhile, discard the onion, garlic and bay leaf and flake the cod into a food processor, discarding any skin or bones.

3. When the potatoes are ready, remove them from the milk with a slotted spoon and transfer to the food processor with the prawns and herbs. Whiz the mixture to a thick puree, adding a little of the cooking milk if needed. Chill the puree in the fridge for 2 hours.

4. Heat the oil in a deep fat fryer, according to the manufacturer's instructions, to a temperature of 180°C (350F).

5. Shape the salt cod mixture into walnut-sized balls and roll them in flour. Cook the fritters in batches for 5 minutes or until golden brown.

6. Transfer the fritters to a kitchen paper lined bowl to blot away any excess oil, then serve immediately with cocktail sticks.

Roast Tomatoes with Cheese and Pesto

8 small tomatoes
50 ml / 1 ¾ fl. oz / ¼ cup pesto
125 g / 4 ½ oz / 1 ball mozzarella, cut into
   16 cubes
2 tbsp fresh basil, shredded
1 tbsp olive oil

1. Preheat the oven to 200°C (180°C fan) / 400F / gas 6.
2. Slice the top quarter off the tomatoes then scoop out and discard the seeds. Fill the cavities with pesto, mozzarella and sprinkle with basil.
3. Heat the oil in an ovenproof frying pan and add the tomatoes. Fry for 3 minutes, then transfer the pan to the oven and roast for 12 minutes. Serve immediately.

Papas Arrugadas

900 g / 2 lb small waxy new potatoes
1 tbsp sea salt

1. Put the potatoes in a single layer in a large saucepan. Pour in enough cold water to almost cover the potatoes, then stir in the salt.
2. Partially cover the pan with a lid and boil for 20 – 30 minutes or until all the water has evaporated and the potatoes are covered by a dusty layer of salt.
3. Leave to rest, uncovered, for 10 minutes before serving.

MAKES: **10** | PREP TIME: **20 MINS** | COOKING TIME: **20 MINS**

Lamb and Chorizo Albondiga Pinchos

50 ml / 1 ¾ fl. oz / ¼ cup olive oil

1 onion, finely chopped

2 cloves of garlic, crushed

250 g / 9 oz / 1 ⅔ cups minced lamb

250 g / 9 oz / 1 ⅔ cups cooking chorizo sausages, skinned

50 g / 1 ¾ oz / ⅔ cup fresh white breadcrumbs

1 egg yolk

a selection of dipping sauces, to serve

1. Heat half of the oil in a large sauté pan and fry the onion for 8 minutes or until softened.
2. Add the garlic and cook for 2 more minutes, stirring constantly, then scrape the mixture into a mixing bowl and leave to cool.
3. Add the lamb, skinned chorizo, breadcrumbs and egg yolk to the onion bowl and mix well. Season with salt and pepper, then shape into twenty meatballs.
4. Heat the rest of the oil in a frying pan and cook the meatballs over a medium-low heat for 20 minutes, turning regularly.
5. Skewer the meatballs together in pairs and serve with a selection of dipping sauces.

SERVES: **4** | PREP TIME: **15 MINS**

Serrano Ham

4 large slices Serrano ham, with a good mixture of fat to lean

1. For the best texture, buy the ham freshly sliced the same day you intend to serve it.
2. Roll up the slices and transfer to a small serving dish.
3. Allow the ham to come up to room temperature for at least 15 minutes.
4. Ideally, it should be served at 21°C (70F).

MAKES: **8** | PREP TIME: **45 MINS** | COOKING TIME: **4 MINS**

Scallop and Bacon Pinchos

16 fresh scallops, shelled and
  corals removed
8 rashers streaky bacon, halved
2 tbsp olive oil
lemon wedges, to serve

1. Soak eight small wooden skewers in cold water for 30 minutes.
2. Wrap each scallop in half a rasher of bacon and thread two onto each skewer.
3. Brush the bacon with oil and season with black pepper.
4. Heat a large heavy-based frying pan until smoking hot, then sear the skewers for 2 minutes on each side, or until the bacon is golden brown and the scallops are only just cooked in the centre.
5. Serve immediately with lemon wedges and a selection of other pinchos.

SERVES: **6** | PREP TIME: **5 MINS** | COOKING TIME: **15 MINS**

Chorizo Caliente

200 g / 7 oz small cooking
  chorizo sausages

1. Preheat the oven to 190°C (170°C fan) / 375F / gas 5.
2. Arrange the chorizo in a single layer in a roasting tin and roast for 15 minutes, turning half way through.
3. Leave the chorizo to rest for 2 minutes before serving.

SERVES: **6** | PREP TIME: **20 MINS** | COOKING TIME: **20 MINS**

Smoked Salmon Pancake Roulades

150 g / 5 ½ oz / 1 cup plain (all purpose) flour
1 large egg
325 ml / 11 ½ fl. oz / 1 ⅓ cups whole milk
2 tbsp butter
150 g / 5 ½ oz / ⅔ cup cream cheese
1 large handful rocket (arugula)
1 small bunch dill, chopped
8 slices smoked salmon

1. Sieve the flour into a bowl and make a well in the centre. Break in the egg and pour in the milk then use a whisk to gradually incorporate all of the flour from round the outside.
2. Melt the butter in a small frying pan then whisk it into the batter. Put the buttered frying pan back over a low heat. Add a ladle of batter and swirl the pan to coat the bottom.
3. When it starts to dry at the edges, turn the pancake over with a spatula and cook the other side until golden brown and cooked through. Transfer the pancake to a plate and cover with a clean tea towel to stop it drying out.
4. Spread the pancakes with cream cheese and scatter over the rocket and dill. Arrange the smoked salmon on top.
5. Roll up the pancakes and cut them into short lengths, securing with skewers. Serve immediately.

MAKES: **10** | PREP TIME: **35 MINS** | COOKING TIME: **20 MINS**

Lamb Albondiga Pinchos

50 ml / 1 ¾ fl. oz / ¼ cup olive oil

2 onions, finely chopped

2 cloves of garlic, crushed

200 g / 7 oz / 1 cup canned tomatoes, chopped

½ tsp smoked paprika

250 g / 9 oz / 1 ⅔ cups minced lamb

250 g / 9 oz / 1 ⅔ cups sausagemeat

50 g / 1 ¾ oz / ⅔ cup fresh white breadcrumbs

½ tsp ground cumin

½ tsp ground coriander

½ tsp ground cinnamon

1 egg yolk

10 slices baguette

1. Heat half of the oil in a large sauté pan and fry the onion for 8 minutes or until softened.
2. Add the garlic and cook for 2 more minutes, stirring constantly, then scrape half of the mixture into a mixing bowl and leave to cool.
3. Add the tomatoes and paprika to the sauté pan and simmer for 10 minutes.
4. Meanwhile, add the lamb, sausagemeat, breadcrumbs, spices and egg yolk to the onion bowl and mix well. Season with salt and pepper, then shape into twenty meatballs.
5. Heat the rest of the oil in a frying pan and cook the meatballs over a medium-low heat for 20 minutes, turning regularly.
6. Arrange the baguette slices on a serving plate and skewer two meatballs to each one. Spoon over a little tomato sauce and serve immediately.

MAKES: **8** | PREP TIME: **5 MINS** | COOKING TIME: **15 MINS**

Chorizo Montaditos

1 tbsp olive oil
8 cooking chorizo sausages
8 slices rustic baguette

1. Heat the oil in a large frying pan and fry the chorizo for 15 minutes over a medium-low heat, turning regularly.
2. Arrange the baguette slices on a serving plate, then top each one with a chorizo sausage and secure with a cocktail stick.
3. Serve immediately.

Three Cheese Croquetas

50 g / 1 ¾ oz / ¼ cup butter
½ leek, finely chopped
50 g / 1 ¾ oz / ⅓ cup plain
  (all-purpose) flour
450 ml / 16 fl. oz / 1 ¾ cups whole milk
75 g / 2 ½ oz / ¾ cup Manchego, grated
75 g / 2 ½ oz / ¾ cup Cabrales, diced
2 tbsp cream cheese
2 large eggs, beaten
150 g / 5 ½ oz / 1 cup fine
  dried breadcrumbs
2 tsp dried oregano
sunflower oil, for deep frying
tomato salsa, to serve

1. Heat the butter in a saucepan and fry the leek over a low heat for 10 minutes. Add the flour and stir over a low heat for 5 minutes, being carefully not to brown it too much.

2. Gradually whisk in the milk, then stir over a medium heat for 12 minutes or until it resembles soft mashed potato. Beat in the cheeses, then spoon it into a piping bag fitted with a large plain nozzle and leave to cool completely. Chill for 2 hours.

3. Heat the oil in a deep fat fryer, according to the manufacturer's instructions, to a temperature of 180°C (350F).

4. Pipe 10 cm (4 in) lengths of the mixture into the beaten egg and turn to coat. Add the oregano to the breadcrumbs, then add the croquetas and turn to coat thoroughly.

5. Deep fry the croquetas in batches for 3 minutes or until golden and crisp.

6. Transfer the croquetas to a kitchen paper lined bowl to blot away any excess oil, then serve immediately with salsa.

SERVES: **6** | PREP TIME: **15 MINS** | COOKING TIME: **5 MINS**

Boquerones Fritos

sunflower oil, for deep frying
450 g / 1 lb / 3 cups fresh anchovies, boned and heads removed
150 g / 5 ½ oz / 1 cup plain (all purpose) flour
lemon wedges, to serve

1. Heat the oil in a deep fat fryer, according to the manufacturer's instructions, to a temperature of 180°C (350F).
2. Season the anchovies with salt and pepper and dredge with flour.
3. Shake off any excess flour, then fry in batches for 5 minutes or until golden brown and crisp.
4. Transfer the anchovies to a kitchen paper lined bowl to remove any excess oil, then serve with lemon wedges for squeezing over.

MAKES: **12** | PREP TIME: **10 MINS** | COOKING TIME: **10 MINS**

Dates Wrapped in Bacon

12 dates, pitted
12 thin rashers smoked streaky bacon

1. Preheat the oven to 200°C (180°C fan) / 400F / gas 6.
2. Wrap each date in a rasher of bacon and secure with a cocktail stick.
3. Arrange the dates in a single layer in a roasting tin and roast for 10 minutes or until the bacon is golden and crisp. Serve immediately.

Ham Platter

100 g / 3 ½ oz / ⅔ cup Serrano ham,
  thinly sliced
4 fresh figs, halved
4 wedges melon
8 small tomatoes, on the vine
4 little gem lettuce leaves

1. For the best texture, buy the ham freshly sliced the same day you intend to serve it.
2. Arrange the ham on a wooden board and allow it to come up to room temperature for at least 15 minutes. Ideally it should be served at 21°C (70F).
3. Surround the ham with fresh figs, melon slices, tomatoes and lettuce.
4. Grind over a little black pepper just before serving.

Chipirones Fritos

sunflower oil, for deep frying
150 g / 5 ½ oz / 1 ½ cups fresh
  white breadcrumbs
½ tsp garlic powder
1 tbsp fresh thyme, finely chopped
1 tbsp fresh parsley, finely chopped, plus
  extra to garnish
50 g / 1 ¾ oz / ⅓ cup plain
  (all-purpose) flour
2 egg whites, beaten until frothy
300 g / 10 ½ oz / 2 cups baby squid,
  cleaned and sliced if large
lemon wedges and tomato sauce, to serve

1. Heat the oil in a deep fat fryer, according to the manufacturer's instructions, to a temperature of 180°C (350F).
2. Mix the breadcrumbs with the garlic powder and herbs in one bowl and put the flour and eggs into two separate bowls.
3. Working in small batches, dip the squid pieces in the flour with one hand and shake off any excess.
4. Dip them in the egg white with the other hand, then toss them into the herby breadcrumbs and use your floured hand to ensure they are thoroughly covered.
5. Fry the chipirones in batches for 2 minutes or until golden brown.
6. Transfer the chipirones to a kitchen paper lined bowl to blot away any excess oil, then transfer to a serving plate and garnish with parsley and lemon wedges.
7. Serve immediately with tomato sauce.

MAKES: **12** | PREP TIME: **30 MINS** | COOKING TIME: **15 MINS**

Monkfish and Serrano Ham Pinchos

200 g / 7 oz / 1 ⅓ cups monkfish fillet, cut into 12 chunks
6 slices Serrano ham, halved lengthways
basil leaves, to garnish

1. Soak twelve short wooden skewers in water for 20 minutes to prevent them from burning.
2. Meanwhile, preheat the oven to 200°C (180°C fan) / 400F / gas 6.
3. Season the monkfish with black pepper. Wrap each chunk of monkfish with half a slice of Serrano ham and secure with the skewers.
4. Roast the pinchos for 15 minutes or until the monkfish is just cooked in the centre.
5. Serve immediately, garnished with basil.

SERVES: 6 | **PREP TIME: 15 MINS** | **COOKING TIME: 5 MINS**

Spiced Whitebait

sunflower oil, for deep frying
200 g / 7 oz / 1 ⅓ cups fine semolina
1 tsp smoked paprika
1 tsp ground cumin
2 tsp dried oregano
450 g / 1 lb / 3 cups fresh whitebait
lemon wedges, to serve

1. Heat the oil in a deep fat fryer, according to the manufacturer's instructions, to a temperature of 180°C (350F).
2. Mix the semolina with the paprika, cumin and oregano and season with salt and pepper.
3. Toss the whitebait with the semolina mixture to coat, then deep fry in batches for 5 minutes or until crisp.
4. Transfer the whitebait to a kitchen paper lined bowl to remove any excess oil.
5. Serve immediately with lemon wedges for squeezing over.

SERVES: 6 | PREP TIME: 45 MINS | CHILL: 2 HOURS | COOKING TIME: 5 MINS

Bacalao Fritters

500 ml / 17 ½ fl. oz / 2 cups whole milk

1 onion, peeled and halved

3 cloves of garlic, squashed

1 bay leaf

200 g / 7 oz / 1 ⅓ cups salt cod, soaked for 24 hours

250 g / 9 oz / 2 cups potatoes, peeled and cut into chunks

1 small bunch parsley, chopped

100 g / 3 ½ oz / ⅔ cup plain (all-purpose) flour

sunflower oil, for deep frying

1. Put the milk in a saucepan with the onion, garlic and bay leaf and bring to a gentle simmer. Lower in the salt cod and simmer for 5 minutes.

2. Strain the milk into a clean saucepan and add the potatoes. Cook for 12 minutes or until the potatoes are tender all the way through. Meanwhile, discard the onion, garlic and bay leaf and flake the cod into a food processor, discarding any skin or bones.

3. When the potatoes are ready, remove them from the milk with a slotted spoon and transfer to the food processor with the parsley. Whiz the mixture to a thick puree, adding a little of the cooking milk if needed.

4. Chill the puree in the fridge for 2 hours.

5. Heat the oil in a deep fat fryer, according to the manufacturer's instructions, to a temperature of 180°C (350F).

6. Shape the salt cod mixture into walnut-sized balls and roll them in flour. Cook the fritters in batches for 5 minutes or until golden brown.

7. Transfer the fritters to a kitchen paper lined bowl to blot away any excess oil, then serve immediately.

SERVES: **8** | PREP TIME: **15 MINS** | SOAK TIME: **36 HOURS** | MARINATE: **2 HOURS**

Marinated Salt Cod

200 g / 7 oz / 1 ⅓ cups salt cod
1 lemon, juiced
50 ml / 1 ¾ fl. oz / ¼ cup olive oil
1 tbsp white onion, finely grated
2 dried red chillies (chilies), sliced
8 slices baguette
½ clove of garlic, unpeeled

1. Soak the salt cod in a large container of water in the fridge for 36 hours, changing the water twice during that time.
2. Drain well, then shred the fish with two forks, discarding any skin and bones.
3. Mix the cod with the lemon, oil, onion and chillies and leaves to marinate in the fridge for 2 hours.
4. Toast the baguette slices under a hot grill and rub the tops with the cut side of the garlic.
5. Drain the cod of any excess liquid, then spoon it on top of the toasts. Secure with cocktail sticks and serve immediately.

Chicken Pinchos Morunos

1 tbsp olive oil
1 tbsp sherry vinegar
½ tsp ground cumin
½ tsp ground coriander
1 tsp smoked paprika
1 tsp cracked black peppercorns
1 clove of garlic, crushed
3 skinless chicken breasts,
 sliced lengthways

1. Mix the olive oil and vinegar with the spices and garlic. Put the chicken in a large freezer bag and pour over the marinade. Seal the bag and massage the marinade into the meat.
2. Leave to marinate in the fridge for at least 2 hours.
3. Meanwhile, soak twelve wooden skewers in cold water for 30 minutes.
4. Thread the chicken onto the skewers and season with salt.
5. Cook the skewers for 3 minutes on each side on a preheated barbecue or under a hot grill. Serve with your favourite dipping sauce.

Pork Pinchos Morunos

1 tbsp olive oil
½ lemon, juiced
½ tsp ground cumin
½ tsp ground coriander
½ tsp ground cinnamon
½ tsp ground turmeric
1 clove of garlic, crushed
350 g / 12 oz / 2 ⅓ cups pork tenderloin,
 cut into strips
pickled vegetables, to serve

1. Mix the olive oil and lemon juice with the spices and garlic. Put the pork in a large freezer bag and pour over the marinade. Seal the bag and massage the marinade into the meat.
2. Leave to marinate in the fridge for at least 2 hours.
3. Meanwhile, soak twelve wooden skewers in cold water for 30 minutes.
4. Thread the pork onto the skewers and season with salt.
5. Cook the skewers for 3 minutes on each side on a preheated barbecue or under a hot grill. Serve with pickled vegetables.

MAKES: **16** | PREP TIME: **15 MINS** | MARINATING TIME: **1 WEEK**

Stuffed Marinated Piquillo Peppers

16 pickled Piquillo peppers, drained, stalks and seeds removed
150 g / 5 ½ oz / ⅔ cup soft goat's cheese, such as Caprichio de Cabra
2 cloves of garlic, unpeeled and gently squashed
1 lemon, zest pared into strips with a vegetable peeler
1 tbsp fresh rosemary, finely chopped
2 tbsp flat leaf parsley, finely chopped
300 ml / 10 ½ fl. oz / 1 ¼ cups olive oil

1. Fill the peppers with goat's cheese and pack them into a jar with the garlic and
   lemon zest, sprinkling in the herbs as you go.
2. Fill the jar with olive oil, then cover and leave to stand at room temperature for
   1 week before serving.

Salads, Sauces and Dips

SERVES: 4 | PREP TIME: 15 MINS

Beetroot and Walnut Romesco Sauce

2 dried Nora peppers

1 clove of garlic, crushed

50 g / 1 ¾ oz / ½ cup walnuts, chopped, plus extra to sprinkle

3 medium cooked beetroot, peeled

1 tbsp sherry vinegar

50 ml / 1 ¾ fl. oz / ¼ cup olive oil, plus extra to drizzle

1 tbsp sour cream

2 tsp mixed seeds

1 tbsp fresh oregano leaves

1. Soak the Nora peppers in boiling water for 10 minutes.

2. Drain the peppers and transfer them to a food processor with the garlic, walnuts, beetroot, vinegar and oil. Add a large pinch of salt and blend to a smooth puree.

3. Spoon the puree into a serving dish and garnish with soured cream and a drizzle of oil. Sprinkle with seeds and oregano leaves and top with a few more chopped walnuts.

SERVES: **4** | PREP TIME: **20 MINS**

Romesco Sauce

2 dried Nora peppers
1 clove of garlic, peeled
25 g / 1 oz / ¼ cup blanched almonds
25 g / 1 oz / ¼ cup walnuts, chopped, plus extra to serve
125 g / 4 ½ oz / ⅔ cup roasted red peppers in oil, drained and chopped
2 ripe tomatoes, peeled, deseeded and chopped
1 tbsp tomato puree
1 tbsp sherry vinegar
50 ml / 1 ¾ fl. oz / ¼ cup olive oil
2 tbsp flat leaf parsley, chopped

1. Soak the Nora peppers in boiling water for 10 minutes.
2. Pound the garlic to a smooth paste with a pinch of salt in a pestle and mortar. Add the soaked and drained Nora peppers and pound until smooth.
3. Add the almonds and walnuts and pound again, then add the roasted peppers and tomatoes. Pound until they break up, but still retain a bit of texture.
4. Stir in the tomato puree, vinegar, oil and parsley and season to taste with salt and pepper.
5. Scrape into a bowl and top with a few more chopped walnuts.

Mozzarella, Olive and Tomato Salad

300 g / 10 ½ oz / 2 cups mozzarella
  ciliegine, drained
200 g / 7 oz / 1 ⅓ cups cherry
  tomatoes, halved
100 g / 3 ½ oz / ⅔ cup black olives, pitted
  and sliced
6 lettuce leaves, torn into pieces
1 tsp dried oregano
olive oil, for dressing

1. Toss the mozzarella, tomatoes, olives and lettuce in a bowl.
2. Sprinkle with oregano and a little salt and pepper and toss again.
3. Serve with olive oil for dressing at the table.

Chickpea and Paprika Dip

75 ml / 2 ½ fl. oz / ⅓ cup olive oil
600 g / 1 lb 5 ½ oz / 4 cups canned
  chickpeas (garbanzo beans), drained
1 clove of garlic, crushed
1 lemon, juiced
½ tsp smoked paprika, plus extra
  for sprinkling
raw vegetable batons, to serve

1. Reserve 1 tablespoon of oil for the garnish and put the rest in a food processor with the chickpeas, garlic, lemon juice and paprika.
2. Blend until smooth, pausing to scrape down the sides as necessary. Season to taste with salt and pepper.
3. Scrape the puree into a bowl then sprinkle with paprika and drizzle over the reserved olive oil. Serve with raw vegetable batons for dipping.

SERVES: **6** | PREP TIME: **5 MINS** | COOKING TIME: **30 MINS**

Tomato, Pepper and Olive Estofado

75 ml / 2 ½ fl. oz / ⅓ cup olive oil

1 large onion, finely chopped

3 red peppers, deseeded and diced

3 cloves of garlic, finely chopped

150 ml / 5 ½ fl. oz / ⅔ cup dry white wine

250 g / 9 oz / 2 cups large ripe tomatoes, peeled, deseeded and chopped

75 g / 2 ½ oz / ½ cup mixed olives, pitted and sliced

1. Heat the olive oil in a sauté pan and fry the onions and peppers over a low heat for 18 minutes, stirring occasionally. Add the garlic and cook for 2 minutes.
2. Pour in the wine and let it boil for 1 minute, then stir in the tomatoes and olives.
3. Cover and simmer gently for 8 minutes, then season to taste with salt and pepper.

SERVES: 6 | PREP TIME: 5 MINS | COOKING TIME: 20 MINS

Tomato and Sweetcorn Salsa

2 tbsp olive oil

1 onion, finely chopped

2 cloves of garlic, crushed

400 g / 14 oz / 2 cups canned
tomatoes, chopped

200 g / 7 oz / 1 cup canned
sweetcorn, drained

1 tsp caster (superfine) sugar

2 tbsp pickled jalapenos, finely chopped

1 tbsp coriander (cilantro), chopped

tortilla chips, to serve

1. Heat the oil in a saucepan and fry the onion for 5 minutes, stirring occasionally. Add the garlic and stir-fry for 2 more minutes.

2. Add the tomatoes and sweetcorn and simmer for 10 minutes, then stir in the sugar and jalapenos. Season to taste with salt and pepper, then leave to cool and chill in the fridge.

3. Scatter the salsa with coriander before serving with tortilla chips on the side.

SERVES: **4** | PREP TIME: **5 MINS**

Chickpea and Tomato Salad

400 g / 14 oz / 2 cups canned chickpeas (garbanzo beans), drained
200 g / 7 oz / 1 ⅓ cups cherry tomatoes, quartered
½ lemon, juiced
50 ml / 1 ¾ fl. oz / ¼ cup olive oil
2 tbsp flat leaf parsley, chopped
2 tbsp basil, chopped, plus a few sprigs to garnish

1. Toss the chickpeas with the tomatoes in a serving bowl.
2. Put the lemon juice and oil in a glass jar and season generously with salt and pepper. Close the lid and shake well to emulsify, then pour it over the salad and stir well.
3. Sprinkle the herbs over the salad and garnish with basil sprigs.

Guacamole

3 ripe avocados, peeled and stoned
1 small onion, grated
1 Jalapeno, deseeded and finely chopped
2 tomatoes, deseeded and diced
1 lime, juiced
tortilla chips, to serve

1. Mash the avocados with a fork until fairly smooth.
2. Stir in the onion, Jalapeno, tomato and lime juice and season to taste with plenty of salt and pepper.
3. Scrape the mixture into a serving bowl and serve with tortilla chips for dipping.

White Bean Dip

75 ml / 2 ½ fl. oz / ⅓ cup olive oil

600 g / 1 lb 5 ½ oz / 4 cups canned white beans, drained

1 clove of garlic, crushed

1 lemon, juiced and zest finely grated

¼ tsp ground cumin

1 tbsp pine nuts, toasted

1 tbsp pumpkin seeds

1 tsp chilli (chili) flakes

flat leaf parsley, to garnish

1. Reserve 1 tablespoon of oil for the garnish and put the rest in a food processor with the beans, garlic, lemon juice and zest and ground cumin.

2. Blend to a textured puree, pausing to scrape down the sides as necessary. Season to taste with salt and pepper.

3. Scrape the puree into a bowl and drizzle over the reserved olive oil. Sprinkle with pine nuts, pumpkin seeds and chilli flakes, then serve garnished with parsley.

Index